ADDRESS

OF

CHARLES H. BELL

BEFORE THE

New Hampshire Historical Society,

ON

MAY 22, 1873;

BEING THE SEMI-CENTENNIAL ANNIVERSARY OF THE FOUNDATION OF THE SOCIETY, AND THE 250TH ANNIVERSARY OF THE SETTLEMENT OF NEW HAMPSHIRE.

CONCORD, N. H.:

PRINTED BY THE REPUBLICAN PRESS ASSOCIATION.

1874.

ADDRESS

OF

CHARLES H. BELL

BEFORE THE

New Hampshire Historical Society,

ON

MAY 22, 1873;

BEING THE SEMI-CENTENNIAL ANNIVERSARY OF THE FOUNDATION OF THE SOCIETY, AND THE 250TH ANNIVERSARY OF THE SETTLEMENT OF NEW HAMPSHIRE.

CONCORD, N. H.:
PRINTED BY THE REPUBLICAN PRESS ASSOCIATION.
1874.

ADDRESS.

Just two hundred and fifty years have passed away since the first permanent settlement of New Hampshire by Europeans was begun. But long before that time, the harbors upon our coast had been familiar to the mariners who yearly ranged the shores of the new world for the spoils of the sea, and who made the acquaintance of the red men by bartering with them the trinkets of transatlantic workmanship for the rich furs which they captured in the forest. Thus the capabilities of the country lying near the coast, and the character and disposition of the native tribes, were well understood, and the first immigrants to New Hampshire were fully apprised of the privations and hardships which they were to encounter. They knew full well that the virgin treasures of the land were only to be won by those who combined the bodily vigor with the resolute will to brave the frosts of winter, and to endure unrepiningly the want of a thousand accustomed comforts, and the absence of friends and congenial society. But with this warning fully impressed upon their minds, they did not hesitate to cast their lot in the remote wilderness. They were attracted hither by the hope of bettering their fortunes, though to many of them the love of novelty and adventure was, doubtless, an additional incentive. The same motives have ever since impelled the hardy pioneers of each successive generation of our countrymen to carry farther and still farther westward the woodman's axe that heads the march of emigration, until at length the broad expanse of the primeval forest is narrowing to a fringe, through which the beams of the declining sun can almost penetrate.

As was to be expected, our early colonists were men of action; in great part, hardy fishermen and lumberers. The waters and the forests, for many long years, yielded them their only resources, and purchased for them in foreign parts the necessaries and the scanty luxuries of which their imperfect agriculture and want of skill in the industrial arts left them destitute. It was not the place nor the life for drones or dreamers; men of thews and sinews, possessors of robust common sense, were the only class who could hold their own in such a campaign against the ever rallying forces of nature. And yet those stalwart pioneers, who abandoned the thousand endearments of social life in the old world, and carved out for themselves homes in the rudest depths of the wilderness, manifested qualities of character which we, in the full light of the present age, enjoying the fruits of a wider experience and higher cultivation, cannot but admire and be proud of.

Their sense of justice in all their dealings with the aboriginal inhabitants is evidenced by the friendly understanding on which they lived side by side with them for half a century, and until other parties and other interests aroused the hostility of the eastern tribes against the whole body of the white settlers. Circumstances, which need not be particularized here, have unfortunately caused the loss and destruction of the greater part of the records and documents of the primary period of the history of New Hampshire; but there is abundant evidence still surviving, to show that every rood of land occupied by the white men for a century after they sat down at Pascataquack, was fairly purchased from the Indian proprietors and honestly paid for.

The early occupants of this soil were singularly free from religious bigotry. The age they lived in was fruitful of dogmatism and persecution, but fortunately no fanatical zeal ever characterized our people. One division of the first permanent company who planted themselves here belonged to the Church of England; yet non-conformist clergymen, in whatever standing with the ruling theology of the Massachusetts Bay, found no hindrance to their ministrations here, with one memorable exception,* for which the people were in nowise responsible. And when New Hampshire had gravitated into substantial accord with the other colonies of New England in her theological views and church polity, it is pleasant to remember that despite the cruel intolerance of the time, no persecutions to the shedding of innocent blood were carried on in the name of religion on this soil. Neither Anabaptist nor Quaker was ever driven to give that crucial evidence of the steadfastness of his faith in New Hampshire. There has come down to us a tradition of a single instance of the infliction of violence in this province for heterodoxy, and that was under the law of Massachusetts; for New Hampshire, as a separate government, never authorized such a penalty. The punishment in that case was cut short by the interference of a person who afterwards made none too creditable a figure as a royal governor of New Hampshire.† But Walter Barefoote deserves to have that one act of mercy, so far in advance of his generation, set down to his credit, in characters of living light. And when the delusion concerning witchcraft, only a score of miles away, was hurrying men, eminent for their learning and piety, into the commission of the most deplorable and fatal errors, we recall with thankfulness the fact that in the few accusations for that offence which were prosecuted in this province, not one reached a tragical conclusion. On the other hand, the records inform us that, in 1669, Goodwife Walford, who had been traduced by the charge of being a witch, boldly brought her defamer into

* Gov. Edward Cranfield, in 1683, instituted a prosecution against Rev. Joshua Moodey, of Portsmouth, for refusing to administer the sacrament according to the mode of the Church of England, as required to do by the governor's order. But Cranfield was not sustained by the people, and at last became so obnoxious to them that he fairly abandoned the province.
1 *N. H. Provincial Papers*, 482, 585.

† In 1662, Richard Waldron ordered three Quaker women to be led at the cart's tail through New Hampshire and Massachusetts, out of the jurisdiction, and whipped in each town. Walter Barefoote, by a pious stratagem, obtained the custody of the women, in Salisbury, and saved them from further cruelty by sending them out of the province.
1 *N. H. Provincial Papers*, 243.

court to answer for the slanderous words, and actually succeeded in casting him in damages.*

Another characteristic of the New Hampshire colonists was their resolute assertion and maintenance of their rights, against the encroachments of cupidity and power. Their trials were far from over, when the wilderness had been subjugated, homes constructed, and order established. New difficulties and dangers then menaced them, not less formidable than those which they had happily surmounted. They were threatened with absolute ruin in the loss of their homesteads and entire landed property. The heir of the original patentee of New Hampshire had now acquired such influence at the British court as to procure a separate administration to be set up for this province, with the avowed purpose of asserting and enforcing his title to all the lands embraced within its limits.

If we could put ourselves in the place of the dismayed inhabitants, we could form a conception how unjust and odious this claim appeared to them. They had heard of John Mason, the patentee, as the person to whom this territory had been granted, under the authority of the king of England, two generations before. The land they believed to have then been worthless, and to have cost him nothing, his object in procuring the title being the hope of profit by setting up fishing and trading posts under it, and by the discovery of precious metals. They understood that after considerable sums had been expended by the patentee, and by his widow after his decease, in establishing agents here and in exploring the country, without any adequate returns, the scheme was abandoned as a failure; and this when next to nothing had been done for the purpose of bringing the soil under cultivation, or promoting its occupancy, or otherwise making it of worth.

On the other hand, their fathers had purchased the lands they lived on from the native proprietors, when there was no other claimant to the ownership known, and had settled upon them in the honest and apparently well founded belief that their occupation could never be disturbed. They had erected commodious dwellings, and tamed the savage forest into arable

* 1 *N. H. Provincial Papers*, 219.

fields, by the expenditure of their own labor and means, and had thus given to the soil all the value which it possessed. The estates so improved and enriched had, in many cases, descended from father to son, or been sold and resold for a full and valuable consideration. Under these circumstances, for the occupants to be ousted from their hard-earned property by the descendant of the first grantee, with a mere paper title, and so little equitable claim of any kind, but especially to the betterments which represented the industry and skill of the colonists, would have seemed a bitter injustice, if done fairly and by due course of law. But when, to enforce his oppressive demand, the claimant was powerful enough to fill the chief offices of the province with interested partisans, and bring the trial of his ejectments before a packed and subservient jury, is it wonderful that the patience of men, whose all was at stake, became exhausted?

The final decision of the great test-suit between the representatives of the patentee and the representatives of the people* has been made the subject of unmerited obloquy. The lawyer of our day, who reads the still existing records, will hesitate long to deny that the defence set up by the landholders was a legal and substantial one; and this irrespectively of the validity of the Wheelwright Indian deed of 1629, which added nothing to the strength of the defendant's case. If that instrument was forged, as has been broadly asserted, to be used as evidence in that suit, it was surely a very supererogatory piece of criminality. The claimant failed to establish his case by reason of the weakness of his own title, and not on account of the strength of that of his adversary. The steadfast resolution with which two successive panels of New Hampshire jurors, in defiance of the illegal restriction which the order of the British queen in council attempted to lay upon their powers, vindicated their constitutional prerogatives by their verdicts, was a fitting sequel to the proceedings, and strikingly exhibited the sturdy spirit of our fathers in upholding their birthright, and in resisting the demands of arbitrary power.

---

* The case of *Allen* v. *Waldron*, the record of which is given in full in 2 N. H. Provincial Papers, 514, *et seq.*

The spirit of liberty, which had always a place in the hearts of our New Hampshire fathers, was aroused as the crisis of resistance to the power of Great Britain drew nigh. It was not that our province had any special material grievance to complain of; on the contrary, our industries were little affected by any acts of the mother country. She had neither sent soldiers to overawe us, nor foreign or hostile officials to rule us. With a royal governor born and reared on our own soil, interested in the prosperity and happiness of the people, and, though faithful to his sovereign, a wise and friendly exponent of his will, New Hampshire made common cause with her sister colonies in opposition rather to the principles than to the practice of tyranny. But, her hand once put to the plow of resistance, she looked not back. One of the earliest armed outbreaks of the people to put down the royal authority was that of the patriots of New Hampshire, when they seized and carried away the arms and ammunition of Fort William and Mary, in the harbor of Piscataqua,* to be used months afterward, against the forces of the king, in that battle which first gave them a wholesome respect for the prowess of the provincials. The first formal constitution adopted in the revolted colonies was that formed and approved by New Hampshire, on the fifth day of January, 1776. The earliest known suggestion on the subject of independence, by an organized body, is found in a letter written by order of the New Hampshire Convention, which was read in the Continental Congress, on the second day of June, 1775.† With what self-denial, courage, and constancy our state performed her part, and more than her part, in the memorable contest that gave to the coming millions of American citizens the birthright of freedom, the pages of history, unfortunately yet unwritten, we trust will one day fitly relate.

It was, in great part, to rescue from oblivion the memorials which still survived of our predecessors on this soil, and of what they effected during the first two centuries after its colonization, that the New Hampshire Historical Society was organ-

* December 14 and 15, 1774.

† Frothingham's Rise of the Republic of the U. S., 421, 422.

ized fifty years ago. It was deemed fitting that so important an anniversary should be observed in some peculiarly memorable fashion; and, therefore, in addition to the literary and festive exercises usual on such occasions, an auspicious beginning was made of a permanent association for historical research;—a monument to the memory of our fathers which, we would fain believe, shall outlast the marble, and bearing inscriptions in their honor which the lapse of ages shall never dim, but, rather, deepen and extend.

The original members of this society were thirty-one in number. We cannot, after the expiration of half a century, read over the list of their names without being profoundly impressed with a sense of their uncommon learning and ability. Some of them died in early life, and never acquired the honors that would later have been at their disposal; but the number of governors, senators, and representatives in congress, doctors of divinity and of laws, and historical writers of no ordinary repute, whom the residue of that little company furnished, is something surprising. It would be no easy task, at this day, to assemble, from the largest state in the union, an equal number of men of like eminence and promise, to engage in an enterprise of this character.

Of the primitive thirty-one, but a solitary individual* survives to witness the fiftieth birthday of the society. Fortunate in the enjoyment of mental and bodily health, he has to-day afforded us auricular, if not ocular, demonstration that his venerable years have neither withered his sympathies nor obscured his powers. He is the connecting link between the infancy and the manhood of our society. We trust that time will long continue, as heretofore, to deal gently with this our last representative of the founders.

Of those who have been the most efficient supporters of the society, there are a few names that it would be inexcusable not to mention on this occasion.

William Plumer was one of the projectors, and the first president of the society. Endowed with a natural fondness for literary and antiquarian pursuits, he bestowed much atten-

* The venerable George Kent, Esquire, now of Washington, D. C.

tion upon them during a large portion of his long life. He collected a great number of documents relating to the state and the nation,—a work for which his long experience in high official positions, and his acquaintance with men of eminence and literary habits, gave him peculiar facilities. At the formation of the society he was past the prime of life, and in such slender health that he never visited the capital of the state after the occasion when he took the presidential chair. He contributed to the first volume of the society's published Collections, and made to the library a handsome donation of desirable books and manuscripts. He retained through life his interest in the society and its work; but his age and the state of his health inclined him to prefer that his son, William Plumer, Junior, should be the active representative of the name in the society. The latter had also been in public life, and possessed a cultivated literary taste. He was one of the publishing committee of the first two volumes of the Collections, and afterwards held the office of president. In 1853, he delivered the annual address, a production of much merit, which has recently found its way, somewhat irregularly, into print.

John Farmer, also an original member, was one of the pillars of our society. Fourteen years in succession he faithfully discharged the duties of corresponding secretary, and he was on the editorial board of four of the volumes of Collections, all of which contained articles from his pen, and one was wholly compiled by him. Mr. Farmer was one of those persons who seem endowed by nature with an aptitude for historical investigation. At an early age he had made himself widely known by his ardor and attainments in that line of study, and they literally grew with his growth. With bodily health so infirm, that, though a resident of the town where the meetings of the society were held, he was not able to attend them more than once or twice during the whole term of his membership, yet his performance of his official services by letter was punctiliously complete; and such were his industry, method, and absorbing devotion to historical and antiquarian studies, that he had accomplished an amount of pains-taking and conscientious work, when the frail thread of his life was broken in his forty-ninth year, which any man might be proud to look back upon after a long lifetime of labor.

The name of Jacob Bailey Moore is naturally associated with that of Mr. Farmer, as they were colaborers in more than one literary and historical enterprise. Their tastes were in many ways congenial, but the firm health and the active and social temperament of Mr. Moore alike forbade him to fall into the secluded habits of his friend. He was the proprietor and editor of a political journal, and his employments led him to make repeated changes of residence, but his popular and genial manners insured him friends wherever he went. He was one of the planners and original members of the society, and served upon the publication committee of two of its volumes, and as librarian. While he continued an inhabitant of the state he rendered yeoman service to the society, and through life his best wishes always went with it. The articles from his pen occupy no small space in the Collections, and are uniformly marked by a spirit of candor, and by careful and thorough investigation.

Richard Bartlett was connected with the society from its inception, and officiated upon the standing committee, and the committee of publication of two of the volumes. He was immersed in active employment, as secretary of the state, a practising lawyer, and a journalist; but he was a warm and constant friend of the society, and lost no opportunity to further its designs and add to its means of usefulness. Almost the last work of his life was the preparation for the society of an elaborate paper on the preservation and keeping of public archives, embracing a great amount of information which he had diligently brought together, accompanied by his judicious comments, which was published in one of our volumes, and in a separate form. At his death, he bequeathed to the society his own library, embracing works of sterling worth, a portion of that of the late Nathaniel Peabody, of revolutionary note, together with a respectable collection of manuscript letters.

Samuel Dana Bell was one of those consulted with regard to the formation of the society, though he did not join it till it had been three years in operation. Throughout his life he habitually appropriated a share of his time to historical study, in addition to the constant performance of his professional and official avocations. His interest in the society was earnest and unceasing. He held the office of president, and served in various other official capacities. He pronounced a carefully prepared annual address, and contributed papers, which bespoke his perfect familiarity with our early history, to the Collections. There came a period of business depression early in the society's existence, when its continuance was imperilled by serious pecuniary embarrassment. Without instant relief, the results of years of labor were liable to be undone. Mr. Bell assumed the pecuniary burden unaided, and carried it till the dawn of better times. It is not too much to say that but for his earnest friendship and constant coöperation, the society could never have attained its present position and repute.

Time will only permit me to make the briefest mention of other members who have contributed in an especial manner to the progress and fame of the society. Levi Woodbury, the occupant of many responsible official positions, state and national, who was the second president of the society, was deeply concerned in its purposes, and delivered a valuable annual discourse. Ichabod Bartlett, the eloquent adocate, in the foremost rank of the profession when the bar of New Hampshire was at its culmination, was the third president, and a contributor to the Collections. Next succeeded to the chair Salma Hale, an accomplished writer and scholar, and a pioneer in one department of school literature. His history of the United States was truly an educational classic, and long retained its estimation with the successive generations of the young, and, more singular still, was repeatedly republished abroad. Mr. Hale sympathized warmly with the objects of the society, and more than once lent his pen to its aid. Charles Humphrey Atherton, who worthily wore a name noted for three generations in our annals, was also numbered among the presiding officers. He was distinguished by his taste for letters and his habits of investigation, and his hand is repeatedly discernible in choice contributions to our printed volumes. Chandler Eastman Potter was also an occupant of the presidential chair, and earnestly solicitous for the welfare and standing of the society. He was a diligent laborer in the field of local history, and has laid an admirable foundation for the compilation of our military annals. His acquaintance with the antiquities of our region, and the manners, language, and policy of the Indian tribes, was exceptionally full and accurate. John Kelly was for the first eight years recording secretary of the society, and in full and warm accord with its designs. He is known to antiquarian students by his numerous sketches, genealogical and biographical, of the early personages of the province, which, in addition to their fidelity to truth, were enriched with a genial humor none the less effective because sometimes wanting in that class of writings. Nathaniel Appleton Haven, Junior, the first corresponding secretary, and one of the projectors of the society, was a cultivated scholar, as well as an ardent student of history. The selection of Mr. Haven to prepare the address on the two hundredth anniversary of the settlement of New Hampshire was a deserved tribute to his gifts and attainments,—as was the assignment of the poem on the same occasion to Oliver William Bourne Peabody, a kindred spirit. Isaac Hill, one of the most vigorous and influential writers of his day, who cherished a regard for everything that promised advantage to the state, found time, in the busiest period of his active life, to serve upon the publishing committee of two of our volumes. Nathaniel Adams and Hosea Hildreth were the earliest members of the standing committee, and were both distinguished in the paths of historical letters. The "Book for New Hampshire Children," composed by the latter, was long a favorite manual in our common schools, and if it were reïssued, and brought up to our own times, would supply a real need in the present course of studies. The names of James Freeman Dana, Nathaniel Gookin Upham, Charles Burroughs, William Cogswell, and other deceased prominent officers and members, crowd upon my pen, and I regret that space does not permit me to allude to them further.

I forbear, for obvious reasons, to mention in this connection any persons now living. Were I at liberty to do so, it would appear that the most efficient friends and benefactors of our association are not all numbered with the dead. It will remain for some future chronicler to do justice to the historical attainments, liberality, and willing personal service of our present members, which have been happily instrumental in placing the society in the prosperous and encouraging position which it to-day occupies.

The results which our society has accomplished, in a life of half a century, we may contemplate with a degree of satisfaction which should cheer us on to continued efforts. It is of course impossible to weigh or to measure the influence which it has exerted in behalf of the acquisition of thorough and exact historical information, not only among its members, but reflectively throughout the community; though there can be no question that this has been wide spread, and of lasting benefit. But there are visible and tangible fruits of its operations which demand a brief enumeration. The society has brought together a library of works for study and reference, for the furtherance of the objects of its constitution, consisting of more than six thousand bound volumes, and twice that number of pamphlets; beside a very considerable quantity of newspapers and manuscripts, Indian, provincial, and revolutionary relics and curiosities. These collections contain many works and objects which are rare, and some unique, bearing upon and illustrating the history of our country, and New Hampshire in particular. Their great value and local importance, and the utter hopelessness of even approximately replacing them in case of their destruction, have led to a determined and persistent effort, within a few years past, to put them within a secure shelter of which the society should be the proprietor. The exertions of several members having the interest of our society much at heart, among whom it is only just that our able and zealous corresponding secretary* should receive special mention, were unsparingly bestowed upon this weighty undertaking. At length, by the generosity of our members, and of the sons of New Hampshire at home and abroad, the desirable object has been effected, by the purchase and adaptation of the handsome, commodious, and secure structure to which you have been so appropriately welcomed this day. The New Hampshire Historical Society is now a freeholder. And no longer are its doors to remain inhospitably closed, but the library and accumulations from this time forward are to be kept open and accessible to all who choose to visit them.

* Rev. Nathaniel Bouton, D. D.

The society has already issued eight substantial octavo volumes of historical collections, relating principally to New Hampshire, and comprising old public and private records, copies of scarce and out-of-the-way tracts, throwing light upon our early affairs, histories of towns, statistics, biographical sketches, and the like. A great part of this invaluable matter was prepared for the press upon the request of the society, and many of the materials would have been irretrievably lost had they not been preserved by the care and foresight of our associates. Nor have these publications been lightly regarded by those for whose use they were intended. They take rank with the best productions of their class. High prices have attested the estimation in which they are held, and the exhausted editions and continued demand for some of the series have compelled the society to reprint two of the volumes; a compliment which will have ere long to be paid to others. The materials for the continuance of these publications are not wanting, so much as the funds available for the purpose. They will soon be renewed, and will be found to decline neither in interest nor in value.

In view of the results thus briefly outlined, we have no cause to be ashamed of the manner in which our society has thus far fulfilled its mission, as set forth in the constitution,—"to discover, procure, and preserve whatever may relate to the natural, civil, literary, and ecclesiastical history of the United States, and of this state in particular."

Our society has now passed the critical stage of its existence. It has encountered and mastered obstacles which, in the nature of things, can probably never present themselves again. The period when it was a novelty and an experiment is over; it is now a fixed institution, and an assured success. Its rare literary possessions, its proprietorship of a commodious hall, the roll of its members, the work it has executed, and the prestige it has acquired, are all proofs of its stability, and pledges of its future prosperity and usefulness.

The work which falls to its lot is of a nature which does not admit of completion. As long as to-morrow shall take the place of to-day, and to-day that of yesterday, so long are time's changes to be recorded, and so long will the demand for our labors never cease. To gather the materials of history will always be one of our chief employments. We are not to be content with heaping our shelves with portly tomes, the works of toil and erudition. They may hold the places of honor, but they are at best but the echoes of the original speech of events. It is the fashion of our time not to take facts at second hand. The authority of even the greatest names is not implicitly accepted. Incredulous inquirers go behind every *ex cathedra dictum* to examine and weigh the evidence on which it is based. Old blunders are exposed; the estimation in which men and their acts were wont to be held is reconsidered, and the verdict of the historian is not unfrequently set aside. Those who assume to instruct the world, no longer dare to trust to the results of others' researches; they must needs go back to the original fountains of information. Every symmetrical storehouse of historical materials, therefore, must supplement the elaborate productions of the annalists with every attainable species of contemporaneous evidence.

There is literally no product of the press or of the pen that cannot be made tributary to the historian's purpose. The lightest bagatelle that springs from the fancy of an hour is as truly the material of history as the ponderous record, imposing in its dignified formality. It is true that, while the latter imports indisputable verity, the other may be obviously amplified to the last degree of exaggeration. Yet both alike convey the truth to him who reads them aright. Nay, the less pretending statement is not seldom more trustworthy than the stately manifesto which has been dressed up for the public eye. Our greatest national historian, when challenged for doing less than justice to some of the prominent characters of the Revolution, has rested his vindication not so much on the public official documents, as on contemporary unpublished memoranda, letters, plans, and chance allusions of eye-witnesses,—evidently believing that from such unvarnished expressions of the sentiment of the hour a juster opinion of the men and their conduct is to be formed than from more elaborate and sophisticated authorities.

While history is thus indebted for its truthfulness to the less pretending walks of literature, they have a special value in imparting to it its picturesque and lifelike aspect. By the judicious chronicler, the brightest and most distinctive reflection of the times he delineates is often borrowed from the trifles which, in their day, were deemed of smallest note,—the artless relations of unlettered men, the freedoms and confidences of private correspondence, the quips and caricatures born of an idle whim. Not seldom furnishing the clue to nice discriminations of character, they are always faithful exemplars of the manners, and redolent of the genuine spirit, of their times. While the warp of history may be drawn from the starched and formal registers, its woof must be fashioned of slighter and more motley stuff, to bring out the quaint patterns and significant designs through which the true genius and character of the age look forth.

The vexatious experience of every one who has undertaken an exhaustive search for the literature pertaining to any subject has taught him that, while the elaborate works are comparatively easy to procure, the difficulty of the pursuit increases in proportion as the productions are trivial, slight in dimensions, and ephemeral in character; broadsides and the like weaklings of the press being only obtainable after the most pertinacious chase. Few persons have any care to preserve the smaller memorials of things passed. Absorbed in the occupations of the day and the cares of the morrow, they abandon to their fate the exuviæ of every event the moment it ceases to be uppermost in their attention.

It is not unfortunate for the cause of knowledge that there exist a small but not unobservant class in the community, who, from pure love to keep green the memory of the persons and things bygone, exercise a protecting care over the waifs which help to a just understanding and appreciation of them. Everything written, printed, pictorial or anywise descriptive, which falls in their way, they carefully preserve. Mementos, which have the flavor of unmistakable antiquity, are their chiefest trophies. But they do not disdain to store up the cast-off rubbish of to-day, because their discernment teaches them that it may become a valued memorial in another generation. But for the indefatigable industry of these thoughtful guardians of the abandoned bantlings of letters, historical societies would be destitute of many of their most interesting accumulations, and the works of historians would lack much of the savor which gives them their piquancy and verisimilitude.

The materials which may be made available for the illustration of New Hampshire history, thus seen to be varied in their character, will be found to be confined to no narrow range. Our province in the early time was so closely associated with other divisions of New England, that whatever illumines the one, necessarily throws light upon the other. In later years our state history is, in like manner, interwoven with that of the country at large. The field for our gleaning is as broad as the boundless continent itself.

Our society has now its representatives so widely scattered, that none of the papers and documents, whether mouldering in the garrets of old mansions, promoted to the collections of tireless antiquaries, or preserved in some other eddy in time's ceaseless stream, which would contribute to the objects of our association, ought to be suffered to miss their way, sooner or later, to our archives. Among those whom interest or curiosity shall draw to our library, it will be strange indeed if some shall not be reminded, by the value we attach to the memorials of by-gone times, to rescue from their forgotten hiding-places historic materials, that would have else perished without a thought. Our fire-proof chambers can hardly fail to tempt the possessors of highly prized hereditary documents, anxious for some place of secure deposit and ready access, to intrust them to our custody. It is not to be forgotten that in our quest, as in all others, nothing is so successful as success. The possessor of ten profitable talents becomes naturally the centre to which all unimproved single talents tend.

But there are higher and more important duties devolving upon our society. We cannot shut our eyes to the fact that but a small proportion even of educated persons manifest an inclination for the studies of history, sufficient to induce them to borrow time for its gratification from their business or their amusements. And particularly is this noticeable in a small state like our own. It is not because of a natural indifference in men to a knowledge of the past;—all our observation of the character of our race forbids such an inference. The desire for information, concerning the generations which have passed away, seems inherent in the human breast. In the earliest times and among unlettered tribes, the knowledge of antecedent events has always been kept alive by tradition; and as man advances in intelligence, his desire to learn is surely not lessened in any direction.

Observation also leads to the conclusion that it is oftener circumstances than the lack of interest which deter men from historical pursuits. It is not common to find a person of intelligence who has not treasured up some facts belonging to the domain of the past, though they be but of family interest or local curiosity. Perhaps he has learned to trace the successive steps of his descent from a Mayflower pilgrim; perhaps he can relate some act of prowess of an ancestor in the Revolution. Or he may point with excusable elation to the name of his first cisatlantic progenitor inscribed on the tattered title of an antique volume, or to the rude engraving of the figures of the chase or the skirmish, executed by a grandsire upon his powder-horn, to while away the tedium of garrison life in the French war.

No one who preserves these relics, with their attendant old-time lore, can be destitute of the historic faculty. The germ of the taste is in his constitution, and it only requires fostering circumstances to cause it to grow and bear fruit. However much cumbered by his cares or his merchandise such an one may be, if he is once brought within the influence of an organized association for historical work he will be attracted to its companionship, and in due time become a competent and useful helper.

Our society has outlived the too prevalent early notion that no one ought to be received into it who had not already achieved distinction. Membership is not regarded, at this day, a reward of merit, so much as an encouragement to exertion. The plan ought to be, to educate our members for our service. Aptitude is important; proficiency is desirable; but active men, in the prime of their powers, holding living relations to the body politic, are indispensable. They are the kind of recruits from whom our most useful veterans of the future are to be fashioned. It is true that we may not find some of them the best adapted for certain dry details of our work;—*non omnes omnia possumus*. But there are other duties to be performed, of equal consequence to the welfare of our organization, which they have the ability, and have abundantly proved their willingness, to undertake. The army of history, like military bodies in general, cannot conduct its campaigns without the sinews of war; and to those of our associates, who give their energies to improve our material resources, belongs no secondary honor.

But the influence of our society should extend beyond the circle in immediate connection with it. It should give tone and direction to the great body beyond. Every project for the discovery and advancement of historical knowledge should receive its encouragement and earnest coöperation. Our people should look to it for instruction and aid in every useful undertaking, and it should never fail to warn them against schemes that are futile or absurd. It is alike our province to promote the publication of the state's invaluable records, and to ridicule the grasping credulity that digs for Kidd's buried treasure, or sets up heirship to a great English estate.

Especially should it be our aim to diffuse a knowledge of the history of our own state, and the biography of its people, as widely as possible in the community. Minute acquaintance with the subject is, of course, not to be expected; but, among the major part of the people, even a general knowledge of New Hampshire's claims to distinction is far less common than it ought to be. New Hampshire is, indeed, one of the smallest divisions of the Union in territory and in population. Her stage of action is a narrow one: none of the great material interests of the country centre within her borders, and her political consequence is trifling. But she has a record to which she may point with pride. Her people have never been wanting in any of the great emergencies, when stout and patriotic hearts were the nation's hope and salvation. When the dusky warriors of the forest threatened the feeble settlements of New England with extermination; when the mercenaries of the English king strove in vain to reduce our struggling country to vassalage; when the strength of the Federal Union was tested by the bloody touchstone of civil war, New Hampshire was alike ready, with her treasure and her blood, to bear her part for the general safety and honor.

It is not possible, nor would it be just, to estimate the achievements of our commonwealth by applying to them the narrow rule of state boundaries. She has given to her sister states and to the country her children, who have largely contributed to their prosperity and power. In every part of our land, from Maine to California, are the sons and daughters of New Hampshire sires to be found. It was no dislike to the land of their birth which impelled them to leave it. They never lose their attachment to their native hills, but always stand ready to reässemble round the homestead, the school-house, and the steeple of their childhood, proud and happy to answer to the roll-call of their parent state. An honorable ambition has led them abroad. In their adopted homes they have achieved their full proportion of the prizes of life. It is not too much to say that prosperity has been the rule with them. Not a few have won an honorable place in the world's regard in science and literature; an unusual share have attained high and influential official positions in other states and in the nation. But we claim them still for New Hampshire. When they went out from us, their places were not made good. All we can have in exchange for them is the honorable names they acquire. Are we to be entitled to no share of the credit which New Hampshire parentage, New Hampshire education, and New Hampshire principles have enabled our children to win on other soil? Are we to give up our claims to the glory of Webster, because the immortal productions of his riper years were uttered outside our territorial lines? Forbid it, Justice! forbid it, Historic Truth! The glory of our children is our glory. No just estimate of New Hampshire can be formed, with the achievements of her absent sons and daughters omitted from the reckoning.

The history of New Hampshire is yet waiting to be adequately written. In the pages of Belknap the provincial period is indeed sketched with a masterly hand; but no light is cast upon the occurrences of the century last past,—the most eventful era of her existence. Within that hundred years the yoke of foreign and monarchical government has been thrown off; nine tenths of her territory has been settled; all her manufactures and communications established; her chief institutions of learning founded, and her literature written.

It is not the province of our society to write history. Nor need our state make any haste to obtain a historiographer. In the fulness of time he will come, with the state pride, the patient industry, the facile pen, the sound discrimination, and the devotion to truth which will adapt him to the task. And then the work which our society has executed will serve its destined office. Congenial spirits among our members will give him their sympathy and encouragement. The contents of our archives will yield him the amplest understanding of his theme. With a mightier magic than that of the tapestry of the Indian prince, they will transport him at a wish into the presence of former generations.

Brethren of the New Hampshire Historical Society: Each step of progress which our organization has taken renders the responsibility of maintaining it in the future more onerous. It has a character to sustain. Whatever increase of effort it may cost, while we remain the guardians of its fame, its onward march must never be suffered to flag, nor its star to be dimmed. Our motto must be,—*Nulla vestigia retrorsum.*

As we return to our homes after these commemorative exercises are over, let us not permit our occupations and cares to crowd the purposes and wants of our society from our remembrance. Whatever service we may be able to render to the cause of historical learning in general, should be ungrudgingly bestowed. But we should bear ever in mind that we are, in an especial degree, bound to promote and foster the interests of New Hampshire history. Everything that will contribute to dignify and adorn it we should cause to be inscribed on the tablets of perpetual remembrance. The good name of our state is the common heritage of ourselves and our children: be ours the grateful office, in our time, to keep it stainless before the world.

www.ingramcontent.com/pod-product-compliance
Lightning Source LLC
LaVergne TN
LVHW012330100826
845148LV00017B/678

* 9 7 8 1 4 2 5 5 7 5 9 4 6 *